The Battle of Bosworth
22 August 1485

❧

D. T. Williams

Lecturer in History
University of Leicester

Leicester University Press
1975

First published in 1973 by Leicester University Press. Distributed in North
America by Humanities Press Inc., New York. Copyright © Leicester
University Press 1973. All rights reserved. No part of this publication
may be reproduced, stored in a retrieval system, or transmitted, in any form
or by any means, electronic, mechanical, photocopying, recording or other-
wise, without the prior permission of the Leicester University Press. Maps
drawn by John Messenger. Designed by Arthur Lockwood.
Set in Monotype Poliphilus. Printed in Great Britain
by Unwin Brothers Ltd, Old Woking, Surrey
ISBN 0 7185 1113 1

Second impression 1975

The site

The site of the Battle of Bosworth has been open to public access since
31 July 1974. Leicestershire County Council have arranged a network of
footpaths with signs explaining the tactics of the opposing forces. Car parks,
picnic areas, information points, a permanent exhibition, an auditorium
for film and slide shows, a diorama, a model of the Battle, and a bookstall
have been provided. The indoor facilities are closed during the winter.
Visitors from a distance may wish to check the times of opening and can
do so by telephoning Leicester 871313 (ext. 435) weekdays only, or they
may write to E. C. Turner, Land Agent, County Hall, Glenfield,
Leicester, LE3 8RR.

O N I AUGUST 1485 the long-awaited but woefully inadequate invasion force commanded by Henry Tudor, Earl of Richmond, set sail from France. What the future king later was to refer to as his "victorious journey" had begun, but the conquest of England seemed a very perilous undertaking for the army of 2,000 hopeful exiles that landed at Milford Haven in Pembrokeshire seven days later. The enterprise was without doubt an act of faith in the loyalty of some very dubious allies. Sir Walter Herbert, King Richard III's representative in South Wales, had been sounded out by the Lancastrians, but so far as Henry knew had not yet committed himself either way. More definite arrangements had been made with secret allies in the north-west, the Stanleys and Gilbert Talbot. Even here there was some doubt. Sir William Stanley, who controlled North Wales, was firmly committed – at least in theory. His elder brother Lord Thomas Stanley, with his usual caution, waited on events. Up to the eleventh hour on Bosworth Field, the Stanleys were to play an equivocal but crucial rôle in what was to follow.
¶ At the moment of landing, Henry sent messengers to the Stanleys and Talbot informing them of his arrival and of his plan to move north through Wales to cross the Severn at Shrewsbury and then, with their support, to move on London. His journey to Shrewsbury, by way of Cardigan, Aberystwyth, and Welshpool, must have taken him about eight days.
¶ Polidore Vergil, the Italian Court historian of the early Tudors, relates that Richard III, at that time near Nottingham, delayed taking any action himself but left matters to his representatives on the spot. This story, quite apart from being entirely out of character for Richard, who was always a man of action, just does not fit the facts. Even if messengers had set out to bring news of the invasion to the King at Nottingham within hours of the landing at Milford Haven, it would have taken the fastest and most stalwart horseman at least four days to cover the 220 odd miles from the Pembrokeshire coast to Nottingham over what must have been some of the most difficult terrain possible. Therefore the earliest Richard could have known of the landing would have been on 10 August. This, in fact, was the day before the first batch of military summons to his supporters were despatched.

The journey ꝫ

¶ One of the surviving letters of array, that sent to the Vernon family, is in itself a most interesting document. Those summoned were ordered to meet the King at Nottingham equipped for war "upon pain of forfeiture unto us of all that ye may forfeit and lose". This salutary warning corroborates the remarks of the Croyland Chronicle to the same effect:

> In the meantime, in manifold letters he despatched orders of the greatest severity, commanding that no men, of the number of those at least who had been born to the inheritance of any property in the kingdom, should shun to take part in the approaching warfare; threatening that whoever should be found, in any part of the kingdom after the victory should have been gained, to have omitted appearing in his presence on the field, was to expect no other fate than the loss of all his goods and possessions, as well as his life.

By the summer of 1485 there was little love between Richard and his subjects. His fear of treachery drove him to rule by fear. The war of nerves waged by the King's enemies throughout the previous 18 months had been successful. Indeed, the King's worst suspicions were to be confirmed by the discovery of yet another conspiracy against him.

¶ Perhaps in anticipation of Henry Tudor's invasion, Lord Thomas Stanley had, shortly before these events, sought permission to leave Court and return to his home in Lancashire. He was allowed to stay there on condition that he sent his eldest son Lord Strange as hostage to the King at Nottingham. The Stanleys must have received news of Henry's landing a day or so before they received their summons from Richard. By that time their military preparations were complete.

¶ Richard, meanwhile, was pleased that the day of reckoning had come. As a born soldier he was at last back in his element. His strategy seems to have been to collect the northern contingents of his army together at Nottingham, then march south to Leicester to join up with his supporters from the south. These included his professional knights of the body commanded by Sir Robert Brackenbury, who garrisoned the Tower of London, and the Duke of Norfolk's force. The latter mustered his retainers at Bury St Edmunds on Tuesday 16 August and marched to Leicester,

2. John Howard, Duke of Norfolk, from an original painting on glass, reproduced from Cartwright's *History . . . of Bamber . . .* , vol. II part ii of Dallaway's Western Division of Sussex. *Photograph by F. M. B. Cooke, University of Leicester.*

arriving a day or so before Richard's Northern army joined them from Nottingham.

¶ Although Richard had sent his summons out to his northern supporters in good time, he was subject to certain delays. The leaders of his two most powerful northern contingents, Lord Thomas Stanley and the Earl of Northumberland, had both been approached by supporters of the Earl of Richmond. Whether by design or by a reluctance to commit himself, Northumberland proceeded to Nottingham at a rather leisurely pace. Lord Thomas, despite the fact that Richard held his son hostage, did not turn up at all, but for reasons that will become apparent later, proceeded via Manchester, Stafford and Lichfield to Atherstone and there camped in a position within easy reach of both converging armies. His force was a powerful one of about 3,000 men.

¶ Richard's own suspicions about the evasive tactics of Lord Thomas were confirmed when Lord Strange, after an unsuccessful attempt to escape, revealed the conspiracy between his uncle Sir William Stanley, Gilbert Talbot and Henry of Richmond. This was a revelation that was sure to compromise even the wily head of the Stanley clan, the cautious Lord Thomas Stanley. It is impossible to unravel the latter's tortuous motives at that point in time, but undoubtedly he suffered agonies of indecision. It was a difficult position for a man to whom equivocation was a cardinal principle of policy. Sir William's position was a little clearer, for Richard proclaimed him a traitor as soon as the details of his connection with Richmond were revealed. But Richard's dark threats to turn Lancashire and Wales into his own private hunting park were directed against the Stanleys in general. Should the invasion fail, they could expect little mercy from their Plantagenet king.

¶ While all this was happening, Henry of Richmond, quite unaware of these complicating factors, was marching along his scheduled route, keeping good time. After successfully crossing the Severn at Shrewsbury, Richmond's line of march veered north-east towards Stafford to link up with Talbot and William Stanley. At first all went according to plan. At Newport, Shropshire, Henry's army, already doubled by his Welsh supporters, was joined on 16 August by Gilbert Talbot and 500 men. In the meantime, Sir William Stanley and about 3,000 mounted

Cheshire men had reached Stone, just north of Stafford, the place scheduled for the link-up with Henry's army.

¶ Because of the difficulties in which he found himself, Sir William delayed his meeting with the future king as long as he could. When it did take place it was not a comfortable one for either of them. The delicate position of the Stanleys and the unmasking of the conspiracy was a severe blow to Richmond, who realized that he and his army, still under 5,000 men, were in a very dangerous position indeed; the more so because even Sir William would not commit himself at this point. All that Henry could salvage from that grim encounter was the promise of a further meeting after Sir William had been in touch with his elder brother. He rode back through the night to Stone, and Henry rode forward empty-handed to rejoin his advancing army, by this time, Friday 19 August, at Lichfield.

¶ After some minor mishaps, Henry and his army arrived at their final resting place before the battle, their camp at Whitemoors (*a*) (letters in parentheses refer to points on the map on the inside back cover, and are listed, with notes, on pp. 23-4), via Watling Street and the Roman Road through Fenny Drayton. The camp itself must have been to the west of the intersection of that road and the one to Shenton. Sir William rejoined his Cheshire men at Stone and they rode hard the following day to meet Lord Thomas and his forces camped near Ratcliffe Culey to the north-east of Atherstone.

¶ The second meeting between Henry and his prevaricating allies took place in a secluded vale somewhere near Atherstone. Although Polidore Vergil states that both William and Thomas attended this second clandestine meeting, it seems more likely that William was again on his own. In a later document, relating to papal dispensation for the marriage between Henry and Elizabeth of York, Lord Thomas stated that he had known Henry personally from 24 August 1485, that is, two days *after* the battle. On this second occasion, Henry must have received a firm commitment of support, and in consultation with Sir William he drew up his battle plan. His most experienced supporter, the Lancastrian Earl of Oxford, was to command the vanguard and centre of Henry's small army, by this time numbering about 5,000 men. Gilbert Talbot was given command of the right wing. The

Stanleys and their combined force of approximately 6,000 men were to make up the left wing, commanded by Henry himself with a much weaker contingent of his own forces. This decision was to be a vital factor in what was to follow. Richmond relied upon the Stanleys to make up the weak left wing of his army. Between them, the Stanleys commanded a force slightly greater than that of the invading army of 5,000. With the Stanleys, Henry Tudor commanded a respectable army of over 10,000 men; without them, his force of 5,000 was obviously inadequate for the task before it. Even at this late stage Sir William did not actually join Henry's army at Whitemoors. Both he and Henry went their separate ways on the understanding that they would join forces the following Monday morning, the 22nd, the day of the battle. Sir William returned to Lord Thomas at Ratcliffe Culey. That night under cover of darkness, unknown to both sides, the Stanleys marched north-east and took up a position on the high ground south of the hamlet of Near Coton (b) overlooking both armies, by that time in the vicinity of Redmoor Plain (c): Henry at Whitemoors, and Richard with a much larger force encamped upon the summit of Ambion Hill, within striking distance of his enemies.

¶ Henry rode back to Whitemoors in better spirits. The Stanleys seemed committed to his cause though there were still some shadows of doubt. These were dispelled for the moment by the arrival in his camp of more defectors from Richard's army. These included John Savage, Brian Sanford, and Simon Digby, with a considerable force of armed men. There had been others. At Tamworth the invading army had been joined by Walter Hungerford, Thomas Bourchier and other former members of Robert Brackenbury's force that set out from London to meet Richard at Leicester. Though few in number, these were valuable as experienced, professional soldiers. Another even more useful adherent was a local man, John de Hardwick, lord of the nearby manor of Lindley, who arrived at Henry's camp the night before the battle, with men and horses. His extensive knowledge of the local topography made him an ideal guide for Henry's army during the critical manœuvres leading up to the battle the following morning. These defectors had brought the strength of Richmond's army to just over 5,000 men on the eve of battle.

¶ It now remains to trace Richard III's progress to Bosworth Field. When the Earl of Northumberland finally joined him at Nottingham, probably on Friday 19 August, the King could delay no longer. It was imperative that he joined Brackenbury and Norfolk waiting for him at Leicester, for his enemies were within striking distance of that town. There is no record of the meeting between Richard and his reluctant ally the Earl of Northumberland, but it must have been a stormy scene. Still, Richard had a large number of loyal Northerners with him, and the following day his powerful force marched in battle order to Leicester, arriving safely at sunset on the Saturday evening, 20 August. The following morning, his army, further streng- thened by the Southerners under Norfolk, Surrey, and Bracken- bury, rode out of the town over the old Bow Bridge, along the Roman Road to Atherstone through the villages of Peckleton, Kirby Mallory and Sutton Cheney (*d*). This was the same road that Henry had taken from the other direction, via Fenny Drayton. At Sutton Cheney, Richard, who had been informed of Henry's whereabouts by his scouts, led his army out along the high ground to the west of the village and camped for the night along the summit of Ambion Hill.

¶ His feelings at this point in time must have been mixed. His army was superior in numbers and artillery to that of his enemy. It is difficult to assess its actual size, because all the sources tend to exaggerate his strength to dramatize Henry's victory. It was probably about 12,000 men, not vastly superior to the combined forces of Henry and the Stanleys, but appreciably so to Henry's army alone. He also had the advantage of the ground. The southern slopes of the little hill were protected by a large marsh (*e*) that ended at the foot of the escarpment leading up to the western side of the hill (*f*). Despite these tactical advantages, Richard had at least two major problems to trouble his sleep that night. His chief worry concerned the loyalty of his troops, particularly that of the forces of the Earl of Northumberland. There had been desertions, not on any large scale, but enough to inflame the nagging suspicions in the King's mind. The second concerned the whereabouts of the Stanleys, who had not yet joined forces with him and who seemed to have disappeared. He could at least take some comfort from the fact that their banners had not been seen in the camp of the Lancastrian usurper below him at Whitemoors. Richard was well aware of the predictable neutrality of Lord Thomas Stanley: he was less sure of the conduct of his brother Sir William, a proclaimed traitor. If, as tradition has it, Richard had nightmares that night on Ambion Hill, they were most likely caused by the impact of these tactical problems upon his military mind.

¶ Before sunrise on the morning of Monday 22 August 1485, Richard and his commanders assembled their men into battle order. When dawn broke, or perhaps after the clearing of an early autumn mist, at least one of the King's problems was solved. From his position on the north-west gradient of Ambion Hill (*g*), Richard could see the Stanleys and their troops drawn up along the high ground to the north straddling the road from Shenton to Market Bosworth. When ordered to do so by heralds, the Stanleys made no move to join Richard's army. Yet they had clearly not joined Henry's either. The King and his commanders regarded them as a potentially hostile force and drew up their battle plan accordingly. The doubtful troops of the Earl of Northumberland were placed in the rearward position defending the steeper northern slopes against the unlikely eventuality of a flanking attack up the hill from the Stanleys. This suited the Earl rather well, for he played no part in the battle that was to follow. The vanguard of the King's army was drawn out in great strength along the vulnerable western slopes of the hill, with the archers to the front as protection against a cavalry charge up the hill. Richard's guns, mainly serpentines, firing a four-pound ball with an effective range of about 1,000 yards, were probably sited on the south side of the van (*h*), protected from a flanking attack by the marsh and chained together to prevent them being ridden down by a frontal cavalry charge. The Duke of Norfolk commanded this, the main body of Richard's army, consisting of perhaps 8,000 men. Richard himself took command of the cavalry, the third and central formation of his force, which was probably sited to the right flank of Norfolk's van, away from the guns, protected by the Duke's screen of men-at-arms and archers, and in a position to charge effectively down the gentler north-western slopes of Ambion Hill into the oncoming enemy.

3. Gothic armour of *c.* 1480: it is a German armour but not unlike those used
in England at the time, most of which seem to have been imported, especially from Italy.
This type of armour was the standard wear of the heavy cavalry of the period.
Crown copyright reproduced with the permission of the Controller of Her Majesty's Stationery Office.

4. Spear head.   5. Hilt of a dagger.   6. Halberd head.

¶ Henry was forced to press home his attack against this formidable defensive position and overwhelming numerical superiority. There is a good deal of truth in the military maxim that no plan can survive the impact of battle. What made Henry Tudor's situation even more precarious was the fact that his plans began to go astray even before his army left its encampment. His commanders drew up their forces according to the prearranged plan early that morning, but the Stanleys did not appear. Moreover, Henry's messenger carrying a request to Sir William to take his place on the left wing of the invading army returned with an ambiguous and non-committal reply. The Stanleys from their vantage point between the two armies were still, at the eleventh hour, waiting on events. This was the first moment of truth for the Lancastrian pretender; there were to be several more before that uncomfortable morning was over. Although appalled by the hopelessness of the situation, Henry and his commanders had only two alternatives before them, either to attack or to be hunted down by a merciless enemy. They chose to attack.

7. Fifteenth-century pivot gun, probably English, and probably from the Loughborough area. *Photographs by courtesy of Leicester Museums.*

¶ At this point it will be useful to know something of the topo-graphy of the battlefield (see map on inside back cover). The most important feature, even more important than Ambion Hill it-self, which was not much of a military obstacle, was the marsh (e). It is the one feature of the landscape mentioned in every detailed account of the battle. It was obviously a large one and it lay between the two armies. The geological features of the hill suggest that without adequate drainage (which was not undertaken till Tudor times) both the north and the south approaches to the hill must have been marshy ground. The bog on the south side was also fed by the spring known as King Richard's Well (i) and others in the vicinity and, perhaps of greater importance, by the Sence Brook that flows through the area. Hutton, who walked the ground in the eighteenth century before the canal was built, wrote that a further marsh existed at that time to the east of the hill, between it and the higher ground to the west of the village of Sutton Cheney. It is therefore reasonable to conclude that the marsh extended right round the eastern and southern slopes of the hill and ended at the rising ground to the north of Bradfields Bridge (j) that forms an escarpment leading up to the western slopes of Ambion Hill. And it was along this, the only vulnerable quadrant in the natural defences of the hill which Henry's army faced, that Richard III, a fine army commander, drew up his van or front line.

¶ Henry assembled his army according to the prearranged plan, Talbot on the right wing, Oxford in the centre and, in the absence of the Stanleys, himself and John Savage commanding an extremely weak and vulnerable left wing. Guided by John de Hardwick, Henry's army advanced in battle order north-east across country to the edge of the marsh. It then turned north-west, following the line of the marsh which afforded protection to his right flank.

¶ It was still quite early in the morning with the sun in the east to the backs of his soldiers as they marched towards Richard's defensive position. Their one consolation was that this line of march also took them towards their reluctant allies, the Stanleys. As they reached the end of the marsh and mounted the higher ground rising to the west, facing the slopes of Ambion Hill, the invaders swung round to meet Richard's van drawn up above them. Talbot paused with his right wing protected from a flanking attack by the marsh. The weak left wing under Henry and the "slender" vanguard and centre under Oxford swung round to the left of Talbot until the entire army stood in line abreast facing the enemy. As had been anticipated, the most vulnerable section was Henry's on the left wing, in a position perhaps facing the present-day site of Shenton Station. This was also the wing of the army nearest to the Stanleys, for by this time Sir William Stanley and his 3,000 Cheshire horsemen in their red coats and badge of the White Hart, accompanied by another 1,000 cavalry from Lord Stanley's retainers, had advanced south towards the battlefield and stopped at a convenient position equidistant from both armies (k). They were still undecided but they were poised to menace the flank of either army. Richard had already made up his mind; orders were given to execute Lord Strange. Fortunately, in the confusion of the battle, they were never carried out.

¶ Once Henry's army had reached the end of the marsh, and while they were engaged in the intricate manœuvre of wheeling round into position, Richard ordered the attack. The four-pounders opened up at effective range, but the fact that their gunners had to fire down the slope probably had some effect upon their accuracy. The showers of arrows from Norfolk's long-bow men at closer range must have taken a deadly toll on Richmond's army. Then, with a shout, the great mass of Norfolk's front charged down the hill upon them. It was a mark of the professional discipline of Henry's army that the wheeling manœuvre was completed in cool deliberation. By the time Norfolk's men-at-arms reached Oxford's vanguard they were in turn assailed by a deadly shower of yard-long arrows drawn at point-blank range.

¶ This impetuous charge down the hill was no blind act of fury, but the move of an experienced and gifted army commander exploiting his opponent's temporary disadvantage and making intelligent use of his vastly superior numbers at the point of attack. His experience of leading the attack against the Lancastrian army at Tewkesbury 14 years earlier had taught Richard the danger of holding an elevated defensive position. On that occasion the close-packed army of Prince Edward had been badly mauled by the missiles of the Yorkist cannons and bowmen, so much so that Richard's attack uphill following the bombardment had been able to breach the Lancastrian front. On Ambion Hill the King had no intention of suffering the same fate by presenting his closely-packed vanguard as a perfect target for the skilful French and Burgundian gunners – at this time the best in Europe – who had been loaned to Henry Tudor by the young Charles VIII of France.

¶ Accordingly, Norfolk's orders must have been to use his overwhelming numbers to charge down, breach, and then envelop the thin, drawn-out vanguard of Richmond's army. However, the Duke met his match in his opposite number, that experienced soldier the Earl of Oxford. Realizing the danger to his slender and extended front line, the Earl planted his Standards in the ground and gave orders to his archers and men-at-arms to shorten their line and not to move more than ten paces from the banners. This command was carried out, and the vanguard drew together in a tightly-packed wedge formation, making it impossible for Norfolk's superior numbers to succeed in the strategy of their attack. In fact, the reverse happened. Fearing some new manœuvre, the King's soldiers drew back to regroup and there was a lull in the fighting.

¶ This was the second moment of truth for Richmond and his army that morning. Richard's tactics had been foiled by the discipline and fortitude of Oxford's archers, pikemen and axemen, and by the professional competence and quick thinking of their commander. Fighting between the two fronts was resumed, but despite the bitter carnage of cold steel at close quarters, Norfolk's soldiers could make little headway against this tightly-packed defensive wedge which had the effect of splitting his force into two wings and so losing the advantage of his numerical superiority. Moreover, any attempt to envelop Oxford's wedge could be effectively dealt with by the two outer wings of Richmond's army. It was probably in this sharp and costly hand-to-hand fighting that the Duke of Norfolk was struck down.

¶ The battle had developed into something of a stalemate for both army commanders. For different reasons, this presented problems to both Henry and Richard. Henry's problem was one of attrition. His vanguard was fighting with discipline, skill and courage but for how long could they sustain the high casualty rate

8. Aerial photograph of the site of the Battle of Bosworth today, taken from the south-east of Ambion Hill looking north of west. *Photograph by P. R. Goodwin, by courtesy of Leicester Museums.*

of such fighting before superior numbers finally wore them down? His one chance was to make a last desperate personal bid to persuade Sir William Stanley to enter the battle on his side with 4,000 fresh cavalrymen. Accompanied by a small bodyguard of under 50 men, Richmond with his Standards unfurled and raised high so as to be recognized by the Stanleys, rode out of the left wing of his army northwards towards them.

¶ Richard's problems were equally serious for, with good cause, he feared treachery in his own ranks. There had been more desertions; Sir William Stanley still remained uncommitted, yet Northumberland sullenly refused to leave his position in the rear when ordered to throw in his weight to reinforce the van now led by Norfolk's son the Earl of Surrey. Time was against the King, for the longer the battle lasted, the greater the risk of desertion or worse. He had to take some initiative to break the deadlock and bring the battle to a swift and successful conclusion. From his position overlooking the battle on the north-west summit of Ambion Hill, the sight of Richmond's banners with their dragon device and the small escort riding with all speed towards the red-coated Cheshire horsemen, must have seemed at once a danger and an opportunity; for he "knew it perfectly by (the) evidence of signs and tokens that it was Henry". Anyone standing in Richard's position overlooking the field can see the opportunity – which he swiftly seized. What happened next, Richard's headlong charge down the gently sloping north-west quadrant of Ambion Hill (*l*) towards his enemy, has been described as an act of impetuous fury and desperate courage. It was a good deal more than that; in fact, a brilliant and almost decisive tactical manœuvre on Richard's part. This charge of 1,000 or more knights, trained from birth in the traditional techniques of chivalrous combat, might not only have overwhelmed Henry's flimsy bodyguard, which it almost did, but also have scattered the weak and vulnerable left flank of his army and driven the exposed centre under Oxford back against the marsh to their right.

¶ As with other master-strokes of strategy, there was a strong element of risk. The attack would have to be pressed home across the front of Sir William Stanley's mounted force, leaving the King vulnerable to a disastrous flanking attack from that quarter. This was a risk Richard was prepared to take, for he knew Lord Thomas Stanley's indecisive and cautious nature. He may not have realized that the Cheshire men were, in fact, commanded by Lord Thomas's less predictable and more impetuous younger brother.

¶ Clasping his shield over his heart, Richard bowed over the high saddletree of his white charger, lowered his lance and, throwing a challenge to his fellow knights, rode headlong down the hill. It must have been a memorable sight, the last real charge of its kind, the swan-song of medieval English chivalry. The tremendous momentum of the attack carried the King and his knights full tilt into Henry's surprised bodyguard. The point of Richard's lance, with the whole power of his charge behind it, transfixed William Brandon, Henry's Standard-Bearer. The King drew his sword and with great fighting skill and courage proceeded to hack his way through to Henry.

¶ This was the third and most crucial crisis in the battle. To the surprise of his experienced companions, the unblooded Richmond fought with cool courage and skill. Although the small group of Lancastrians fought well, they would quickly have been

overcome by the force and the scale of that magnificent charge.
¶ It was also the moment of truth for Sir William Stanley. If he
did not act immediately the battle was lost and he would face
the consequences of his treason against King Richard. After a
moment's hesitation, perhaps looking for an agreed signal from
his elder brother some way to the north, Sir William led his 4,000
Cheshire men straight into Richard's flank with the cry "A
Stanley, A Stanley".
¶ The impact of this flanking attack dramatically reversed the
critical situation for Henry Tudor. Richard was unhorsed and
his companions brought him another to flee the field. This he
valiantly refused to do and charged once more into the hopeless
fight to be cut down by his enemies near the spot where the little
stream passes under the present Sutton Cheney to Shenton
road (*m*). The comment of a contemporary, John Rous, is the
best epitaph on Richard's death as a soldier.

> If I may speak the truth to his honour, although small of body
> and weak in strength, he most valiantly defended himself as a
> noble knight to his last breath often exclaiming that he was
> betrayed . . .

¶ From that point on, the field was Henry's. Northumberland,
witnessing the attack by Sir William Stanley from his vantage
point on the north slopes of Ambion Hill, instinctively retired
north with troops who had played no part in the battle. His
neutrality during this critical encounter reflected his conduct 14
years earlier during Edward IV's victorious invasion of 1471. On
this occasion, as on the previous one, inactivity was enough to
earn the gratitude and favour of the victorious king. It seems
likely that the weapons found near the Sutton Cheney to Bosworth
road in 1748 were those discarded by his foot soldiers, by then in
full flight.
¶ The Southerners under the Earl of Surrey, realizing that the
battle was lost, broke off their bloody engagement with Oxford
and, again instinctively, fled south across Redmoor Plain in the
direction of Stoke Golding, following the remnants of Richard's
own mounted knights driven in that direction by Sir William
Stanley's flanking attack. They were pursued by the victorious
army as far as Stoke Golding, where tradition has it Henry

Epilogue 🐗

mounted the small hill, later called Crown Hill, and thanked his brave companions-in-arms. Richard's crown, or rather the gold diadem he wore on his helmet, had been found on a thorn-bush (or more likely under it, placed there by a dishonest but quick-witted soldier) by Reginald Bray. It was taken to one of his commanders who placed it on Henry's head to the cheers of the victorious army. England had found a new king, Henry VII.

¶ The body of the old one was stripped, thrown over the back of a horse and, with his beloved White Boar Herald before him bearing his Standard, poor Richard's mangled remains were carried back to Leicester. His naked body covered with the blood and mire of battle was displayed publicly for two days in the Newarke before being claimed by the Franciscan Friars for burial. The treatment of Richard's remains perhaps reflected his bad reputation as king south of the Trent. It was also a deliberate act of policy by the new king.

¶ The death of Richard III began a centuries-long debate about his character and reputation as king. The positions taken by those involved in that debate reflect the changing fashions and politics of our national history. At the turn of the fifteenth century, however, opinions upon the last Plantagenet king were often a reflection of the differences between those who lived in the north, and those who lived in the south of England. The sorrow inspired by Richard's death amongst his northern subjects is perhaps best summed up in this extract from the minute book of the Corporation of his beloved city of York, within a few days of the battle:

> . . . king Richard late lawfully reigning over us through great treason . . . with many other lords and nobility of these northern parts, was piteously slain and murdered to the great heaviness of this city. . . .

The less enthusiastic verdict of his southern subjects finds expression in the Great Chronicle of London:

> . . . thus ended this man with dishonour as he that sought it, for had he continued still protector and have suffered the children [of Edward IV] to have prospered according to his allegiance and fidelity, he should have been honourably lauded over all, where as now his fame is darkened and dishonoured as far as

he was known, but God that is all merciful forgive him his misdeeds.

Between them, these comments contain the known truth about Richard, but the verdict of history is still an open one.

¶ So far, we have followed the way of kings, the sordid and unedifying path that led to Henry VII's close-fought victory at the Battle of Bosworth. Henry always regarded his elevation to the throne as an act of Divine intervention. There is indeed something rather miraculous about his rise from the forgotten exile of 1483 to the throne of England two years later. The truth was that his fate rested on a knife-edge right up to the last stages of the battle on the morning of 22 August 1485. He owed his crown to the last-minute intervention of the Stanleys, who were to reap morally unjustifiable rewards for their final, last-minute duplicity. But there were others who were the real unsung heroes of Bosworth Field, the tough, professional soldiers who made up Henry's "slender" vanguard. What kind of men were they, and how did they fight?

¶ These questions are not answered in the various accounts of the battle itself, but there is some near-contemporary evidence from much further afield. The year after the battle, one of Henry's Yorkist supporters, Lord Scales the Earl Rivers, who had fought at Bosworth, travelled to Spain with 100 archers and 200 men-at-arms from his retinue to join the last European crusade, the Conquest of Granada. Some of his retainers must also have been veterans of Bosworth Field, perhaps all of them. Friar Antonio Agapida, who wrote the Chronicle of the Conquest of Granada, an impartial observer, had this to say about the nature and fighting qualities of these English warriors:

> This cavalier was from the island of England, and brought with him a train of his vassals; men who had been hardened in certain civil wars which had raged in their country. They were a comely race of men, but too fair and fresh for [the appearance] of warriors. They were huge feeders, also, and deep carousers; and could not accommodate themselves to the sober diet of our troops, but must fain eat and drink after the manner of their own country. They were often noisy and unruly, also, in their wassail; and their quarter of the camp was prone to be a scene

of loud revel and sudden brawl. They were withal of great pride; yet it was not like our inflammable Spanish pride; . . . their pride was silent and contumelious. Though from a remote, and somewhat barbarous island, they yet believed themselves the most perfect men upon earth. . . . With all this, it must be said of them, that they were marvellous good men in the field, dexterous archers, and powerful with the battle axe. In their great pride and self will, they always sought to press in their advantage, and take the post of danger. . . . They did not rush forward fiercely, or make a brilliant onset, like the Moorish and Spanish troops, but went into the fight deliberately and persisted obstinately, and were slow to find out when they were beaten.

The friar, in a later passage, comments upon their conduct in the field during the siege of the Moorish city of Loja. He first of all describes the appearance of Earl Rivers himself going into battle, and then continues:

He was followed by a body of his yeomen, armed in a like manner [that is, with swords and battle axes] and by a band of archers with bows made of tough English yew tree. The earl turned to his troops and addressed them bluntly according to the manner of the country. 'Remember my merry men all', he said, 'the eyes of strangers are upon you: you are in a foreign land, fighting for the glory of God and the honour of Merry Old England!' A loud shout was the reply. The earl waved his battle axe over his head. 'St George for England', he cried. They soon made their way into the midst of the enemy but when engaged in the hottest of the fight, they made no shouts or outcries. They pressed steadily forward dealing blows right and left, hewing down Moors, and cutting their way with their battle axes like woodmen in the forest; while the archers, pressing into the opening they made, plied their bows vigorously, and spread death on every side.

¶ These were the professionals who stood their ground on the western slopes of Ambion Hill in the face of overwhelming odds; it was their obstinacy and fighting skill at a crucial phase of the battle that won the throne of England for the Tudor dynasty.

(*a*) According to a local but ancient tradition, Henry Tudor and his army camped on the eve of the battle to the south-west of Ambion Hill in the meadows to the west of the road leading into the village of Shenton from the south. Today the site of the camp known as Whitemoors is marked by a covert of trees. Before dawn on the morning of 22 August 1485, Henry's commanders drew up their forces in order of battle, probably on the flat ground to the south of the camp itself.

(*b*) The small community of Near Coton is situated on the ridge of the high ground that rises to the north of Ambion Hill in the direction of Market Bosworth. The Stanley forces were, therefore, situated in a commanding position overlooking both Ambion Hill and Whitemoors, the lower-lying ground to the west of it. Of equal importance for the events of the morning of the battle, their position and strength were clearly visible to King Richard and his army from their vantage point on the summit of Ambion Hill.

(*c*) The area within the confines of Market Bosworth to the north, Sutton Cheney to the east, Stoke Golding to the south and Upton to the west, was known in the fifteenth and sixteenth centuries as Redmoor Plain. As the entire action of the battle from the initial manœuvres to the final rout took place within this locality, not surprisingly, it became known as the Battle of Redmoor. According to the seventeenth-century antiquarian, Burton, the name was changed much later to the Battle of Bosworth, as Bosworth was the most important town and landmark in the immediate vicinity.

(*d*) That both Richard III and Henry Tudor turned off the old Roman Road they had previously followed, the King at Sutton Cheney, the Earl on to the track leading to Shenton, suggests that in the fifteenth century the large marsh that skirted the southern slopes of Ambion Hill may have extended eastwards making the adjacent portion of the old road quite impassable for an army and its equipment. This conjecture, which would account for the positions of the two armies on the eve of the battle, is supported by a close study of the topography, drainage and field names of that area. The Tudor chronicler Holinshed, who may have had personal local knowledge, commented that the greater part of this marsh was drained and reclaimed during the sixteenth century.

(*e*) An examination of the geological features of Ambion Hill and of the lie of the land below it, suggests that this extensive and impenetrable marsh skirted the southern and eastern slopes of the hill. It was without doubt the major topographical obstacle of the battlefield that may have determined the actual site of the battle itself. This took place on the rising ground above and beyond the mire which led up to the west-facing slopes of Ambion Hill.

Notes

(*f*) From time to time throughout the intervening centuries, cannon balls of stone and iron have been unearthed on this western sector of the hill in the environs of Glebe Farm.

(*g*) This vantage point overlooking both the Stanleys and the left wing of Henry's army is indicated by a sign on the Hill itself.

(*h*) Their most likely location was to the south of Glebe Farm protected by the marsh and Norfolk's vanguard. Richard's guns were most probably serpentines which were carried on horse-drawn carts and set up on pivots or spikes. There is a good deal of evidence to show that Richard had a considerable arsenal of these guns in the Tower of London and others stored in his chief strategic fortresses throughout the kingdom. Serpentines were perhaps the most versatile and transportable field artillery pieces of this period in use in England.

(*i*) A monument to Richard III was first erected above this spring in the early nineteenth century, and has been restored and refashioned from time to time. The latest and most harmonious restoration has been carried out by the White Boar Society.

(*j*) The name given to the present-day bridge that carries the road from the former Shenton Station south-east to Sutton Cheney across the canal below Ambion Hill.

(*k*) The probable location of Sir William Stanley's mounted force is indicated on the map.

(*l*) The terrain must have been quite suitable for such a charge. As an experienced field commander, Richard III most certainly took into account the lie of the land and positioned his mounted force accordingly.

(*m*) Henry VII's proclamation issued within a few days of the battle, stated that Richard was slain "at a place called Sandeford within the shire of Leicester". This spot was most probably the ford where the present Sutton Cheney to Shenton road that runs below the northern slopes of Ambion Hill, passes over a small brook, in a position between the embankments of the canal and the railway.